FAITH IN CHRIST INFERRED FROM FAITH IN GOD

FAITH IN CHRIST INFERRED FROM FAITH IN GOD

In a Sermon Preached at the Tuesday Lecture, at Salters Hall, May 29, 1711

୶

REV. MATTHEW HENRY

MINISTER OF THE GOSPEL IN CHESTER

Ye believe in God, believe also in me.—JOHN 14:1

CURIOSMITH
MINNEAPOLIS

Published by Curiosmith.
Minneapolis, Minnesota.
Internet: curiosmith.com.

ISBN 9781946145123

GUIDE TO THE CONTENTS
———oo⚫oo———

FAITH IN CHRIST INFERRED FROM FAITH IN GOD

Ye believe in God, believe also in me.—JOHN 14:1.

A dominion over your faith[1] is what your ministers are far from pretending to; but the direction of your faith is what they are intrusted with, that thus they may be *helpers of your joy*, for *by faith you stand*. What is Paul himself, or what is Apollos,[2] those great men? not masters in whom ye believed, but ministers only, by whom ye believed; not oracles, but stewards of the oracles of God. Now how can we better direct your faith, nay, how dare we otherwise direct it, than as we have received direction from the Lord Jesus, who is the Author and Finisher of our faith, the Foundation and Fountain of it? And in the text we have his law concerning it, the rule of faith he prescribes to us. What he said here to those who were his immediate

1 2 Corinthians 1:24.
2 1 Corinthians 3:4.

followers, he says to all, *Ye believe in God, believe also in me.*

This is here recommended in particular to the disciples of Christ; as a sovereign antidote against trouble of mind, proper to fortify the soul against the invasions of grief and fear, when they are most violent and threatening, and all other supports and succors fail. Christ was now leaving those who had left all to follow him, and he told them that whither he went they could not follow him yet;[1] which seemed to bear hard upon them, that they who had followed him in his sorrows, might not follow him to his joys; nay, must be left behind as sheep in the midst of wolves. Because of this, *sorrow filled their heart.* And though in Christ's departure from them there seems to be enough to justify their sorrow, yet there really is enough to pacify; and therefore, with good reason, as well as with good authority, he commands down those boisterous winds and waves, saying, *Peace, be still.* Let the sinners in Zion be afraid, and let fearfulness surprise the hypocrites, but let not your hearts be troubled. Though trouble surround you on every side, yet be wise, be watchful, and keep trouble from your hearts: and that you may do so, *believe in God,* and in his providence; *believe also in me,* and in my grace. And you will be kept from fainting by believing;[2] but if you will not

1 John 13:36.
2 Psalm 27:16.

believe, surely you shall not be established.[1]

But that which is here intended as a cordial in time of trouble, will not be so, unless it be our practice, for it is certainly our duty at all times, the duty of all those who hear the joyful sound of the everlasting gospel, not only to believe in God, but to believe also in Jesus Christ. And therefore I shall take it more generally, not only as an antidote against trouble of mind, but a caveat against practical deism.

1. Our Lord Jesus does here take it for granted concerning his disciples, that they did believe in God, and that in the belief of him they paid him the adorations due to his name, and the submissions due to his government, and that that faith was so firmly fixed in them, that it would not be shocked by any event of Providence, though ever so grieving, ever so frowning. *You believe in God*, that is, you receive and embrace natural religion, you admit the light of it, you submit to the laws of it. You believe the perfections of God, that he is infinitely and eternally wise and holy, just and good; you believe his relations to his creatures, as their Protector and Benefactor, their Owner and Ruler; his relations to his own people, as their Father and Felicity; you believe his providence, that it extends itself to all the creatures, and all their actions, to you, and all your affairs, with a certain cognizance,

1 Isaiah 7:9.

and a faithful steady conduct. Nay, you go further, you not only believe in the Lord your God, but you believe his prophets[1] you receive the Scriptures of the Old Testament, and subscribe to them: and you do well. Observe here,

(1.) That our Lord Jesus knows who believe in God, and who do not; for all hearts are open to his view, and he knows what is in man. When with the mouth confession is made unto salvation,[2] it is to give honor to him, not to inform him what the heart believes; for he knows it before we tell him, and better than we can tell him. That which is the prerogative of the Eternal Mind, is one of the flowers of the Redeemer's crown: *I am he which searcheth the reins and hearts*.[3] He knows the sincerity of some, whom men suspect and reproach, and the insincerity of others, whom men confide in and applaud. We read of some who professed to believe in Jesus Christ, when they saw the miracles which he did; but *Jesus did not commit himself to them*, did not *believe* them, so the word is, *because he knew all men, and needed not that any should testify of man*.[4] He knew that his disciples here did believe in God, and witnessed for them that they did so. And because he does thus infallibly know

1 2 Chronicles 20:20.
2 Romans 10:10.
3 Revelation 2:23.
4 John 2:23–25.

every man's true character, he is therefore fit to be the Judge of all at the great day, and to pass the definitive sentence upon every man's everlasting state; for we are sure that his judgment is according to truth, and cannot mistake.

(2.) That our Lord Jesus is highly well pleased with those who believe in God, and will take notice of it to their comfort and honor. He came into the world to reveal and reconcile God to us, and to reduce and restore us to God, not to draw us *from* him, but to draw us *to* him; and nothing is more acceptable to him than our believing in God, nor shall any thing be more comfortable to us. Christ fortifies us with this faith against all assaults: *Let not your hearts be troubled*, for ye *believe in God*. And those who believe in God need not be cast down and disquieted; as those have reason to be who are strangers to him, who have no dependence on him, or communion with him. They who believe in God, according to his word, have reason to rejoice in him with joy unspeakable; for their confidence in him shall not *make them ashamed*. They *know whom they have believed*.

2. He calls upon them who believe in God, to believe in him too. But did not the disciples believe also in Christ? No doubt they did; else they had not so easily left all to follow him, and continued with him in his temptations. When St. Peter, in the name of the rest, gave this for the reason why they

would never quit their Master, *We believe and are sure that thou art the Christ, the Son of the living God,*[1] they all subscribed to it as the confession of their faith, except Judas, whom Christ at that very time particularly excepted. And yet, Christ saith to them, *Believe also in me:* use the faith you have, set it on work, exert it, employ it, that by it you may keep your minds composed and quiet at this time. *Believe in me,* that is, live by faith in me. Even those who believe, as they have need to be prayed for, that God would help their unbelief, and increase their faith, so they have need to be preached to, and called upon to exercise their faith: *These things are written to you who believe* in Christ, *that you* MAY *believe* in him;[2] may be confirmed in your faith, and have the comfort of it.

Believing in God is a very great duty, and there are few but what profess at least to do it. They who have little else to say for themselves, will say this, "We trust in God": and O that there were *such a heart* in all them that say so! But from those who believe in God, there are two things further required: *One* is a dictate of the light and law of nature; we have it given in charge by St. Paul to Titus, *This is a faithful saying, (and these things I will that thou affirm constantly;*[3] let it be frequently inculcated,

---

1 John 6:69.
2 1 John 5:13.
3 Titus 3:8.

and earnestly pressed upon all Christians), *That they who have believed in God must be careful to maintain good works:* for *faith without works is dead;*[1] *it doth no good to others,*[2] and therefore will do *us* no good.—The other is a dictate of revealed religion, and we have it here in the text, "Ye believe in God, *believe also in me."*

> Doctrine: It may justly be expected, and required, from those who believe in God, that if they are within the sound of the gospel, they should believe also in Jesus Christ.

I speak to those who are favored with the gospel, who see that joyful light, who hear that joyful sound, and who are therefore concerned in this doctrine. As for those who enjoy it not, we cannot say it is required of them to *believe* in Christ; for *how shall they believe in him, of whom they have not heard?*[3] Yet we cannot say, it is impossible for any of them, though they live up ever so closely to the light they have, to be saved by Christ they never heard of. It is *out of our line* to judge concerning them, for it is not *in our Bibles;* but let us judge this rather, that we who enjoy the gospel shall find it more intolerable for us in the day of judgment, than they will, if we obey not the gospel. As for them, it becomes us rather to leave them to God's

1 James 2:17.
2 James 2:14.
3 Romans 10:14.

uncovenanted mercy, than to his unpacified justice. For our own part, whatever favor they may find who are destitute of the light of Christianity, I see not how they can expect it, who rebel against that light, and reject the counsel of God against themselves.[1] The case is plain—It is *good* to believe in God; but that is *not enough*, we must believe also in Jesus Christ. It is not sufficient to our acceptance with God that we embrace natural religion, though it is indispensably necessary that we do so; but we must go further, we must admit the light, and submit to the laws, of the Christian religion likewise, which is consonant to, and perfective of, natural religion, and helps us out where that leaves us at a loss. And this is that which I am here today to press upon you, with all seriousness, that you sink not into a practical deism, as many do into a practical atheism; but, in every thing wherein you have to do with God, you may have a believing regard to Jesus Christ. *You believe in God, believe also in Jesus Christ.*

I shall here endeavor to explain,

I. The *objects* of this faith, and what that is which those who believe in God are to believe also concerning Christ.

II. The *acts* of this faith, and what that regard is which we must give to God, and must give also to Jesus Christ.

III. The connection between these two, and how

_____
1 Luke 7:30.

necessarily it follows, that those who truly believe in God will readily believe in Jesus Christ, when he is made known to them. And then make application.

I. Let us inquire, *what* man is to believe concerning God; and compare with that, *what* he is also to believe concerning Jesus Christ; and see, *what relation they have* to each other.

1. Do we believe in God, as the *Father Almighty?* We must believe in Christ, as his *only-begotten Son;* for Father and Son correlates. By the prescribed form of baptism, that great foundation on which the doctrine of the Trinity is built, we are directed to devote ourselves to the Father and Son; which plainly speaks a divine relation, not to us, (for though God may be said to be a Father to us, and a Holy Spirit to us, yet he can in no sense be said to be a Son to us), but a relation to one another; and therefore they must be distinct persons; and so, as that the Son is the *express image of the Father's Person.* We cannot believe in God as the *Father,*[1] but we must believe in him who is the *Son of the Father,*[2] who is the *only-begotten of the Father,*[3] and therefore of the same nature with him. If any *deny the Son,* though they say they believe in God, as the Creator of heaven and earth, yet really *they have not the Father,* they have not the knowledge of him,

1 Hebrew 1:3.
2 2 John 3.
3 John 1:14.

nor an interest in him, as the *Father;* for they only who by faith continue in the *Son,* so continue *in the Father.*[1] Shall we think that God has the title of the Father ascribed to him so frequently, so solemnly, only as he is the Fountain of being to the creatures which are infinitely below him? (So the heathen called him the Father, so he is *Father of the rain, and hath begotten the drops of the dew.*[2]) No, he himself plainly intimated why he is called the *Father,* when he said to the Redeemer, *Thou art my Son, this day have I begotten thee;*[3] which must be understood in a far higher sense than that of creation; for when the apostle would prove that Christ has obtained a more excellent name than the highest rank of created beings, he thus argues: *To which of the angels said he at any time, Thou art my Son, this day have I begotten thee?*[4] They were *sons of God* who *shouted for joy, when the foundations of the earth were fastened;* he was the *Image of the invisible God,* that existed *before all things.*[5] It is not, as some would have it, that he WAS *flesh,* and WAS MADE *God,* only as Moses was made a god to Pharaoh; for the Scripture says quite the contrary, that θεος ην—*he* WAS *God,*[6] and

---

1 1 John 2:23, 24.
2 Job 38:28.
3 Psalm 2:7.
4 Hebrews 1:5.
5 Colossians 1:15, 16.
6 John 1:1.

σαρξ εγενετο—WAS MADE *flesh*.[1] This mystery we firmly believe the *truth* of, but awfully adore the *depth* of.

2. Do we believe in God as the *Eternal Mind?* We must also believe in Christ as *the Eternal Word and Wisdom*. God is an Infinite Spirit, and as such is to be adored by every one of us; and he has told us that the Redeemer we are to believe in is the *Logos*, that *in the beginning, was with God; and was God*,[2] in the constitution of all things. And (to show that he is the *Omega* as well as the *Alpha*) we find that in the consummation of all things, when he obtains a final victory over all the enemies of his kingdom, he appears and acts under the same title; his name is called, *the Word of God*.[3] It signifies both *Ratio* and *Oratio*, a word *conceived*, and a word *uttered*. Christ is both; as the thought is one with the mind that thinks it, and yet may be considered as distinct from it, so Christ was and is *one with* the Father, and yet *distinct* from the Father.

In all the divine counsels, Christ is the *Eternal Wisdom*, that when God *prepared the heavens*, and *laid the foundations of the earth*, and made man who is *the highest part of the dust of the world*, was *by him as one brought up with him:*[4] he is the

---

1 John 1:14.
2 John 1:1.
3 Revelation 19:13.
4 Proverbs 8:26, 30.

Wonderful Counsellor, in whom are *hid all the treasures of wisdom and knowledge*. Between the Father and the Son there is a perfect mutual consciousness, and particularly in the affair of man's redemption. *No man knows the Son but the Father, neither knows the Father, save the Son*.[1] The counsel of peace is between them both.[2]

In all divine revelations, Christ is *the Word* of the Father; that Word of God which is quick and powerful, and is a discerner of the thoughts and intents of the heart.[3] He only having lain in his bosom from eternity, none but he could declare him;[4] and though it is in these last days, that he has in more especial manner spoken to us by his Son, yet the Spirit, in the Old-Testament prophets, was the Spirit of Christ.[5] And as he was the Maker and Mediator, so he was the *Messenger of the Covenant*, the *Amen*, the *faithful and true Witness*.

3. Do we believe that *God made the world, and governs it?* We must believe also that he made it, and governs it, by his Son, who is not only the *wisdom of God*, and his eternal word, but the *power of God*, and his almighty *right hand. The Father worketh hitherto;*[6] we believe he does, that he is

1 Matthew 11:27.
2 Zechariah 6:12.
3 Hebrews 4:12.
4 John 1:18.
5 1 Peter 1:11.
6 John 5:17, 19.

the Fountain of all being, and the Spring of all life, power, motion, and perfection: but the Son has told us withal, that he worketh, and that *what things soever the Father doth, these also doth the Son likewise.*

Nothing appears more evident, by the light of nature, than that God made the world, and all things therein, that by his power, and for his pleasure and praise, they are and were created: nor does any thing appear more evident, by the light of the Gospel, than that God *made the worlds by his Son,*[1] that he *created all things by Jesus Christ,*[2] *that all things were created by him and for him,* and that *he is before all things, and by him all things consist,*[3] nay, *that without him was not any thing made that was made.*[4] So that if we receive the gospel, we must discern even in the things that are seen, not only the eternal power and godhead of the Father, but the universal agency and influence of the Son, and particularly with reference to the children of men, with whom his delights were; for in him, in a special manner, was that *life which is the light of men.*[5] Therefore he is called the Ἀρχη—*The principle* (so it might better be read than *The beginning*) of the

---

1 Hebrews 1:2.
2 Ephesians 3:9.
3 Colossians 1:16, 17.
4 John 1:3.
5 John 1:4.

creation of God.[1] And hence arises his sovereignty over all the creatures, and his property in them. He is *the first-born of every creature;*[2] that is, as the apostle himself explains it, he is *the heir of all things;*[3] and has not only by purchase, but *by inheritance, obtained* the *more excellent name.*

We are satisfied that God governs the world, and an abundant satisfaction it is to us that he does so, that his kingdom ruleth over all; but we must also be assured, and it will add greatly to our satisfaction, that the administration of the kingdom of providence is put into the hands of our Lord Jesus, and is united to the mediatorial kingdom; that he has an incontestable title to all, *All things are delivered to him by the Father,*[4] and for this reason, because *he loves him,*[5] that he has an uncontrollable dominion over all. Things are not only given into his hand, but put under his feet;[6] not only great power, but all power, is given unto him, both in heaven and in earth; and he is not only head of the church, but *head over all things to the church.* All the angels in heaven are his active servants, all the devils in hell are his conquered captives: the kingdoms of the

---

1 Revelation 3:14.
2 Colossians 1:15.
3 Hebrews 1:2, 4.
4 Matthew 11:27.
5 John 3:35.
6 Matthew 28:18.

earth are his, and he is the Governor among the nations;[1] *By him kings reign*, for to him the Father has committed not only the future judgment, but *all judgment.*[2]

4. Do we believe that God is our owner by right of *creation?* We must believe also, that Christ is our owner by right of *redemption;* and yet we have not two masters to serve; Christ and the Father are one, as to us. Nor do these properties stand in competition with each other: no, Christ owns his property to be derived, *Thine they were, and thou gavest them me,*[3] and yet withal it is acquired.

As to God we owe our *being*, because he made us, and not we ourselves, therefore we are not our own but his; so to Christ we owe our *well being*, our recovery from that deplorable state, unto which by sin we were fallen, and our restoration to the favor of God, and an eternal happiness in him. Thus, besides the original right he has to us as our Maker, he has an additional right by purchase; a right to command us, a right to dispose of us; we are his servants, for he has loosed our bonds; not only born in his house, but bought—not with his money indeed, but with that which is infinitely more valuable, his own most precious blood: and therefore we are delivered out of the hands of our

---

1 Psalm 22:28.
2 John 5:22.
3 John 17:6.

enemies, that we might be devoted to him, to serve him without fear.[1] We are not our own but his, for *we are bought with a price;* more was paid for us a great deal than we were worth; and it was paid to him into whose hand our all was forfeited, so that no dispute can be made of his interest in us, and the authority he has to demand our best affections and services. As *one is our Father,* even God, so *one is our Master, even Christ:*[2] he is our Lord, and we are bound to worship him.[3]

5. Do we believe that God is our *Judge,* to whom we must every one of us give an account of ourselves? We must believe also, that Christ is our *Advocate* with him, and that he is the *propitiation for our sins.* We are all conscious to ourselves that we are sinners, that we are guilty before God, have incurred his wrath, and laid ourselves open to his curse; and from him our judgment must proceed, a judgment against which there will lie no exception, and from which there will lie no appeal; a judgment which in its inquiries will look back as far as our beginning, for *God shall bring every work into judgment, with every secret thing:*[4] and which in its *decisions* will look forward as far as our everlasting state, which must by it be irreversibly determined.

---

1 Luke 1:74, 75.
2 Matthew 23:8, 9.
3 Psalm 45:11.
4 Ecclesiastes 12:4.

Now, whenever we think of giving an account to God, we must have an eye to the Lord Jesus, as the one only Mediator between us and God, that blessed *Days-man* who has *laid his hand upon us both;* who is *our peace*, who arbitrates matters in variance between us and God; who takes up the quarrel, slays the enmity, and, in whom God was so far reconciling the world unto himself, as that all those who perish in the quarrel, have their blood upon their own heads. And he is our Advocate, who having *made* peace for us, *speaks* peace for us in the intercession which he EVER *lives to make*, in the virtue of the satisfaction he ONCE FOR ALL *died to make*. It is he who interposed between us and God, by whom God speaks to us, and we plead with God; who appears for us, acts for us, answers the charges exhibited against us, and sues out the blessings purchased for us, and promised to us. This is his office, and he attends continually to this very thing.

6. Do we believe that *God is our end*, and that in his favor our happiness is bound up? We must believe also, that *Christ is our way*, and that we cannot obtain the favor of God, but in and through him. If we know ourselves, and the nature and capacities of our own souls, we cannot but know that he who made us, is he whom we are made for, and is alone able to make us happy, and not the world, which was made for us; that he who is the Fountain of our being, is the alone Felicity of it;

that his loving-kindness is therefore better than life, this natural life, because it is the life of the soul, it is our spiritual and eternal life.

It is certain those are happy whom God loves; but the question is, how we poor sinners may come at this happiness? The gospel will resolve that question, for it tells us that Christ is the *true and living way* to the Father;[1] the old way, the new way, the only way: that there is no coming to God as a Father, but by Jesus Christ the Mediator. That he is the door by whom we enter into covenant and communion with God; that he is the light to guide us in the way; that he is our High Priest, who is *ordained for men in things pertaining unto God*, and, as the forerunner, is for us entered; that it is by him that we have access to God,[2] are introduced into his presence, and recommended to his favor and grace, and may come boldly to the throne of his grace: and as such a one we are to believe in him.

II. I come now to show, that the acts of this faith in Christ must be the same with the acts of our faith in God. The same word is used concerning both, signifying the same thing. We believe in God, we must believe also in Jesus Christ; that is,

1. *We acquaint ourselves with God*, we must *acquaint ourselves also with Jesus Christ*. Grace and peace are multiplied to us through the knowledge

1 John 14:6.
2 Ephesians 2:18.

of God and of Jesus our Lord,[1] through that faith which arises from right knowledge, and presses after more knowledge; for as knowing is necessary to our believing, so believing is necessary to our further knowing. We think we are concerned to know the only true God; we are so, but that will not be life eternal to us, unless withal we know Jesus Christ; whom he has sent,[2] to acquaint us with him, and lead us back to him, and make us happy in him. It is the knowledge of Christ which blessed Paul saw such a transcendent excellency in, and for which he was willing to suffer the loss of all things:[3] he desired, he *determined to know nothing but Christ, and him crucified,*[4] because he knew that Christ's death is our life. Those therefore are grossly ignorant of God and themselves, (however they may boast of their knowledge) who desire not to be acquainted with Jesus Christ, but make light of the knowledge of him. Let us then who follow on to know the Lord, follow on to know the Lord Jesus, to know yet more and more of him. We know something of God by the light of nature, but much more by the light of divine revelation; and by that light we come to the knowledge of Jesus Christ too: so that in studying that, we get and grow in the knowledge

---

1 2 Peter 1:2.

2 John 17:3.

3 Philippians 3:8.

4 1 Corinthians 2:2.

both of God and Christ, that is, of *the glory of God in the face of Jesus Christ.*[1]

2. We adore *God,* we must also *adore Jesus Christ.* They who believe in God as a being infinitely bright, and blessed, and glorious, and the Sovereign Lord of all, will see themselves obliged to give him the glory due to his name, and to profess their faith in him, by paying their homage to him, and seeking to him for mercy and grace. And thus we must express our faith in Christ, as that blind man, the eyes of whose mind were opened with those of his body; and then he said to Christ, *Lord, I believe; and he worshipped him.*[2] It is the will of God that *all men should honor the Son, even as they honor the Father*, that they should give him divine honors, as one with the Father. And our confessing that he is Lord redounds to the glory of God the Father, whose person he is the express image of.[3] All the angels of God were appointed to worship him,[4] even when he was brought into this lower world,[5] and they did so. Much more reason have we to do it, now he is entered into his glory, we who lie under greater obligations to him than the angels do. And every creature is brought in ascribing the same

---

1 2 Corinthians 4:6.
2 John 9:38.
3 Philippians 2:11.
4 Hebrews 1:6.
5 Luke 2:14.

blessing, and honor, and glory, and power, both *to him that sits upon the throne and to the Lamb*.[1] Do we express our faith in God by praying to him? We do so; for as we cannot call on him in whom we have not believed,[2] so we cannot but call on him in whom we have believed. Thus, therefore, we must express our faith in Christ, we must pray to him, as many did when he was here upon earth, and none in vain. It is made the description of Christians, that they *call on the name of Jesus Christ our Lord*,[3] because they trust in that name. Stephen testified his faith in Christ, when he prayed, *Lord Jesus, receive my Spirit*.

3. *We stand in awe of God*, we must also *stand in awe of the Lord Jesus*. Faith and fear go together; Noah by faith was moved with fear. If we believe the majesty of God, we shall tremble at his presence, and be afraid of falling under his displeasure, much more of remaining under it. Let us also believe in Jesus Christ, and thus express it. Let us have awful thoughts of him, and of that authority which he is invested with, as Lord of all, and our Judge. Let us rejoice in him with a holy trembling, and kiss the Son with a religious fear, lest he be angry, and we perish from the way,[4] and be undone for ever; lest

---

1 Revelation 5:13.
2 Romans 10:14.
3 1 Corinthians 1:2.
4 Psalm 2:11, 12.

we be found among his enemies, that he will order to be brought forth and slain before him; among those rebels who shall be tormented *in the presence of the holy angels*,[1] *and in the presence of the Lamb*,[2] even he looking on and reckoning himself glorified in the final rejection of those who rejected him. For whether he be feared now or no, the day is coming when even the great and mighty men would be glad to hide themselves, not only from the face of him that sits upon the throne, but from the wrath of the Lamb;[3] finding to their confusion, that this Lamb is the *Lion of the tribe of Judah*, whose wrath more than that of any earthly king is as the *roaring of a lion*, and as *messengers of death*. Justly therefore is the kingdom of the Messiah introduced with this command, *Fear before him all the earth*,[4] for he is great, and greatly to be feared.

4. We *study to do the will of God;* all who believe in him do so; we must also *study to do the will of Jesus Christ*, and in the temper of our minds, and the tenor of our lives, to comply with it. Faith in God produces obedience to him. Those do not really give credit to his promises, whatever their professions and pretensions are, who are not willing to come up to the conditions of them; for so truly

---

1 Luke 19:27.
2 Revelation 14:10.
3 Revelation 6:16.
4 Psalm 96:9.

rich, so very rich, are the blessings proposed, and so very easy and reasonable are the duties required, to which those blessings are annexed, that those who will not be brought to the duties, must be looked upon as not believing either the truth of the promise, or the value of the things promised. But those who really believe that *God is, and that he is the rewarder of them that diligently seek him,*[1] will set themselves to seek and serve him; and thus faith in Christ will produce obedience to him. It is for the obedience of faith that the gospel is made known to all nations;[2] and it is in vain to call Christ Lord, if we do not the things that he saith;[3] in vain to call him our King, if we conform not to the laws, and serve not the interests, of his kingdom; in vain to expect from him the privileges of adoption, if we do not, as obedient children, fashion ourselves[4] according to the spirit of his family, and the rules by which it is governed. If we do indeed believe in Christ as the *author of eternal salvation to all those that obey him,*[5] and to those only, and believe that salvation is from everlasting misery, and to everlasting blessedness, surely we shall make no difficulty of obeying him, yea, though his precepts be

---

1 Hebrews 11:6.
2 Romans 16:26.
3 Luke 6:46.
4 1 Peter 1:14.
5 Hebrews 5:9.

to deny ourselves, and to take up our cross daily.[1]
If we do indeed believe that Christ loved us and
gave himself for us, and that we owe our all to his
love, surely it will be an easy thing to us to love
one another,[2] in conformity to his example, and
in obedience to that new commandment which he
has given us. If we do indeed believe that Christ
sits at the right hand of God, and has there prepared a place for us,[3] we shall thereby find ourselves strongly engaged to set our affections on
things above.

5. We *delight ourselves in God*, and rejoice and
triumph in him; we must *also delight ourselves in
Jesus Christ*, and rejoice and triumph in him. *We
believe in God*, and therefore take a complacency
in him, in contemplating his beauty, participating
of his bounty, and in the relishes of that benignity
of his, which is better than life. Our souls not only
return to him, and repose in him as their rest, but
please themselves in him as their *exceeding joy*—the
gladness of their joy,[4] so the word is. And thus we
must make it appear that we believe also in Jesus
Christ; we must take a pleasure, a transcendent
pleasure, in the views of his loveliness in himself,
and his love to us. Our meditation of God must be

---

1 Matthew 16:24.
2 John 13:34.
3 Colossians 3:1, 2.
4 Psalm 43:4.

sweet, and so must our meditation of Jesus Christ: we must love to think of him, as of one we love and have an interest in. They are the circumcision,[1] they are indeed the children of the covenant who rejoice in Christ Jesus;[2] who in his name lift up their banners; who glory in the Lord,[3] who glory in his cross, so far are they from being ashamed of it. In him shall *all the seed of Israel be justified;*[4] and, as a fruit and evidence of it, *in him they shall glory,*[5] in him as *The Lord their righteousness.*

If, believing, we rejoice in God,[6] believing, we must rejoice also in Jesus Christ; for in him dwell not only all the awful, but all the amiable, perfections of the divine nature. Is God light? Christ is the light of the world, and a pleasant thing it is with the eye of faith to behold the Sun of Righteousness. Is God love? in nothing does it more appear that he is so than in sending his Son to die for us: in him he commended his love.[7] Nor could we, in our guilty and polluted state, delight ourselves in a just and holy God, no, nor think of him without terror, if there were not a Mediator between us and him. It is in Christ Jesus that we rejoice, and in God through him.

1 Philippians 3:3.
2 Psalm 20:5.
3 1 Corinthians 10:3.
4 Galatians 6:14.
5 Isaiah 45:25.
6 1 Peter 1:8.
7 Romans 5:8.

6. We depend upon God, and put our confidence in him; let us also depend upon Jesus Christ, and put a confidence in him. We believe in God, that is, we trust in him, we rely upon his wisdom to direct us, his power to support and strengthen us, his goodness to pity us, and his all-sufficiency to give all that *to us*, and work all that *in us*, and *for us*, which the necessity of our case calls for. And we therefore refer ourselves to him, and encourage ourselves in him; now let us thus believe also in Jesus Christ, and make him our hope. As we confide in the providence of God for all things that relate to the natural life; and cheerfully submit ourselves to the conduct of that providence, hoping by it to be carried comfortably through this world; so we confide in the grace of the Lord Jesus for all things relating to the spiritual life, and cheerfully submit ourselves to the operations of that grace, hoping by it to be carried safely to a better world; desiring not more to secure our present and future welfare, than to have the *grace of the Lord Jesus Christ with our Spirit*.[1] Our dependence must be upon Christ both for righteousness and strength,[2] the two great things we stand in need of; from a full conviction of our own guilt and weakness, and of his ability and willingness to save us from sin and wrath, we must venture all our spiritual concerns with him. In every thing wherein we have to do with God, we must make mention of

---

1 Galatians 6:18.
2 Isaiah 45:24.

his righteousness, and make use of his grace—and, of both, as all-sufficient for us; must depend upon him to bring us safe through this wilderness to the heavenly Canaan; and having done this, as those who know whom we have trusted, we must be willing to venture all our temporal concerns for him, to leave, and lose, and lay out all for his sake, being well assured, that though we may be losers for him, we shall not, we cannot, be losers by him in the end.

III. I come in the next place to show the necessary connection that there is between these two great duties, of believing in God, and believing also in Jesus Christ; and how the latter will follow of course, if the former be sincere, in all those to whom the glad tidings of the gospel-salvation are brought. They must needs embrace the Christian religion, who cordially entertain natural religion; and they who do not believe in Christ, whatever they pretend, do not indeed believe in God: for,

1. If we *believe in God*, we must believe in him who is *One with him, the Brightness of his glory*, and *the express Image of his Person*.[1] Christ in his gospel has expressly told us, *I and my Father are one*.[2] And when he says, *My Father is greater than I*,[3] the comparison is not between the person of the Father and of the Son, but between the Son's state of

---

1 Hebrews 1:3.
2 John 10:30.
3 John 14:28.

exaltation with the Father and his present state of humiliation; as *plainly* appears, because it comes in as a reason why the disciples should not mourn, but rejoice rather, in his departure from them, because he had told them he was to go to the Father, where his state would be not only more glorious to himself, but of greater capacity to serve them, than his present state was. When he was entering upon his sufferings, he comforted himself with this, that *he and his Father were one, Thou, Father art in me and I in thee,*[1] and therefore he has reason to expect, that *the world will believe*, that *they who believe in God*, will believe also in him. So much are the Father and the Son *one,* that Christ says, *He that has seen me, has seen the Father.*[2] We come to the knowledge of God, by the knowledge of Jesus Christ, for the glory of God shines in the face of Jesus Christ; and, therefore, he who believes in the *Father*, as far as the *Son* is revealed to him to be one with the Father, will believe also in him: and by that faith we come to be one *with* the Father and the Son, and one *in* them.[3] And thus, by keeping Christ's commandments *we abide in his love*, even as he kept his Father's commandments, and *abode in his love.*[4] Such a close and inseparable union the gospel all along shows us

1 John 17:21.
2 John 14:9.
3 John 17:21.
4 John 15:10.

between the Father and the Son, as that we cannot divide them in our belief. The heathen worshipped their idols as rivals with God, we worship Christ as one with God: *Believe me*, says Christ, that *I am in the Father, and the Father in me.* So let us believe in him.

2. If we *believe in God*, we must believe also in him who is *sent by him*, has a *commission from him*, and to whom he has *given testimony.* We do not believe in God, unless we believe what he has said concerning his Son, and rest upon it; what he said by the prophets of the Old Testament, who all bare witness to him. And those predictions of theirs were all exactly and completely accomplished, which had reference to his estate of *humiliation*, and the afflictions of it; not one iota or tittle of them fell to the ground. Christ himself observed this when he said, *It is finished:* which ratifies those predictions that had reference to his estate of *exaltation*, the honors of it, and the graces that flow to us from it; for *the Spirit of Christ, in them, testified beforehand* both *of the sufferings of Christ, and of the glory that should follow.*[1] We must also believe, what he said by a voice from heaven concerning him, once and again, *This is my beloved Son, in whom I am well pleased, hear ye him;*[2] and must concur with him by a sincere declaration, *This is my beloved* Saviour,

1 1 Peter 1:11.
2 Matthew 3:17.

in whom I am well pleased, and whom I will hear.[1]
Thus we set to our seal that he is true,[2] and subscribe to the record we have received in the everlasting gospel, which we are willing to venture our
souls and our salvation upon, that *God has given to
us eternal life,* and *this life is in his Son;* which if
we receive not make God a liar,[3] we not only declare
that we do not believe in him ourselves, but that he
is not fit to be believed by any one else. Justly therefore has Christ said, *He that despiseth me, despiseth
him that sent me;* as an affront done to an ambassa-
dor, is justly construed an affront to him who gave
him his character and credentials.

We must also, if we believe in God, give credit
to the many confirmations which we have of his
testimony to his Son; the many miracles which
were wrought to prove his divine mission, miracles
of mercy, healing mercy, which served likewise to
explain and illustrate it; especially the resurrection of Jesus Christ from the dead, by which he
was declared to be the Son of God with power,[4]
and in which God gave him glory, that our faith
and hope might be in God;[5] that believing in him
whom he raised from the dead, our faith and hope

---

1 Matthew 17:5.
2 John 3:33.
3 1 John 5:10, 11.
4 Romans 1:4.
5 1 Peter 1:21.

in him might be both evidenced and encouraged. The pouring out of the Spirit likewise, both in his gifts and in his graces, is a further attestation given to Christ's mission, for in them God bare him witness;[1] nay, the Holy Ghost whom God gave to them who believed in Christ, and obeyed him,[2] is said to be his witness; so that if we believe in the Spirit of God, we must believe also in Christ, and, therefore, the imputing of Christ's miracles, which were wrought by the Spirit of God, to Beelzebub the prince of the devils, is justly reckoned an *unpardonable blasphemy against the Holy Ghost*.

3. If we *believe in God*, we must *give honor to him*, by *believing also in Jesus Christ;* for thereby he reckons himself honored. If *we confess that Jesus Christ is Lord*, it is to the *glory of God the Father*.[3] It is certain, there is nothing in which the glory of God, and of all his attributes, shines more bright, or more strong, than in the great work of our redemption wrought out by Jesus Christ; and therefore, when the First-begotten was brought into the world, the angels who were charged to worship him sang, *Glory to God in the highest*, because, in Christ, there was *on earth peace, and good-will, towards men*:[4] so that, unless by faith in Christ we receive that peace

---

1 Hebrews 2:4.
2 Acts 5:32.
3 Philippians 2:11.
4 Luke 2:14.

and good-will, and the record given concerning it, we do not as we ought give unto God the glory due to him, from that greatest of all the works of wonder by which he has made himself known. Do we believe in God? We ought then to give him the glory of all that infinite wisdom which contrived our redemption in such a way, that divine justice might be satisfied, and yet sinners saved; this is the *wisdom of God in a mystery, hidden wisdom, manifold wisdom, ordained before the world for our glory.*[1] We ought also to give him the glory of that kindness and love of God which designed this salvation, those tender mercies, whereby the Dayspring from on high visited us; love without precedent, love without parallel, whereby God so loved the world, as to give his only-begotten Son for us. But how can we say we believe in him, which is giving glory to him, if we rob him of so great a part of his glory, by not believing in Jesus Christ, in whom his glory shines in a special manner?

4. If we *believe God speaking by Moses and the prophets*, we must believe also in Jesus Christ; for to him bare all the prophets witness, and in all the ceremonies of the Mosaic institution, he was typified: if we believe the Old Testament, we must also believe the New; for such an exact correspondence and agreement is there between them, as between two tallies. The same grace which the Old

1 1 Corinthians 2:7.

Testament represents in shadows, promises, and predictions, the New Testament produces in the substance and accomplishment, so that they mutually confirm and illustrate one another. This our Lord Jesus insisted upon, as one of the strongest proofs of his divine mission, that the Scriptures of the Old Testament *testified of him;* and therefore he tells the Jews, who set up Moses in opposition to him, that Moses, instead of condemning him, condemned them for not believing in him; for, says he, *Had ye believed Moses, ye would have believed me, for he wrote of me.*[1] In *the volume of the book,*[2] εν κεφαλιδι—*in the head* of it, (so the word is) in the very beginning of the book of Moses, it was written of Christ, that as *the seed of the woman*, he should *break the serpent's head*. It is plain, therefore, ye *believe not his writings*, because ye *believe not my words*. Christ blamed the two disciples, and afterwards all the rest, for their slowness to believe what was written concerning him in the law of Moses, and in the prophets, and in the Psalms, all which was to a tittle fulfilled in him.[3] They who believed in the God of Israel, and received the oracles which by him were committed to them, knew very well that there was a salvation to be revealed in the last times; that a Messiah should come, to be a prophet

1 John 5:45–47.
2 Hebrews 10:7.
3 Luke 24:25, 27, 44.

like Moses, a priest like Aaron, a king like David—and, like the sacrifices, to make reconciliation for iniquity; and that he should be cut off, not for himself, but for the sins of his people.[1] And do we not see all this abundantly made good in the Lord Jesus? Has he not done, has he not suffered, all that which it was foretold he should do and suffer? If, therefore, we believe that a Messiah was to come, we must believe that *this was he that should come, and we are not to look for any other.* The apostles therefore all along appealed to the Scriptures of the Old Testament, *saying no other things than those which Moses and the prophets said should come,*[2] and putting the unbelief of the Jews to their ignorance of *the voice of the prophets,* though they were *read among them every sabbath day.*[3] So that, in short, if we believe that there is such a thing as a divine revelation, that God has made a discovery of himself, and of his will and grace, to the children of men, we must believe the gospel, and the testimony it bears, *God has sent his son into the world, not to condemn the world, but that the world through him might have* righteousness and life.

5. If we rightly apprehend how matters stand between God and man since the fall, as those must do who believe in God, who believe his holiness

1 Daniel 9:26.
2 Acts 26:23.
3 Acts 13:27.

and justice, and his relations to man, we shall readily receive the notice which the gospel gives us
of a Mediator between God and man; not only
because we shall soon perceive how desirable it is
that there should be such a Mediator, (and we are
easily brought to believe what is for our honor and
advantage, *quod volumus facile credimus—what
we wish we easily believe*) but because we shall
perceive, likewise, how probable it is that a God
of infinite grace and mercy should appoint such a
Mediator, and make him known to us. It is a great
confirmation of the truth of the Christian religion,
that it not only agrees with, and is a ratification of,
the principles and laws of natural religion, and is
an improvement and advancement of them, but
that it supplies the deficiencies of it; it takes us up
and helps us out, where that fails us and leaves us
at a loss. So that if we make just reflections upon
ourselves, and our own case as it appears to us by
the light of nature, there cannot but be a disposi-
tion in us to receive and embrace the gospel, and to
entertain it not only as a faithful saying, but as well
worthy of all acceptation, that Christ Jesus came
into the world to save sinners. If we rightly believe
in God, and withal rightly understand ourselves,
we cannot but perceive our case to be such as calls
for the interposition of a Mediator between us and
God; and we are undone if there be no such a one;
and we will therefore cheerfully receive him.

(1.) We cannot but perceive that man has in a great measure lost the knowledge of God, and therefore should gladly believe in him who has revealed him to us. It is certainly the greatest satisfaction and best entertainment to our intellectual powers, to know God the author and felicity of our beings. The understanding of man cannot *rest* short of this knowledge; but we find that by the entrance of sin, our understandings are darkened,[1] and the children of men are generally alienated from the divine light and life, through the ignorance that is in them, because of the blindness of their heart: *The world by wisdom knew not God,*[2] and *the things of God are foolishness to the natural man.*[3] Are we sensible of this as our misery, that we cannot by any researches of our own come to such a knowledge of God, as is necessary to our communion with him? If we are so, we shall readily embrace Christ as a prophet, who having lain in the bosom of the Father from eternity, has declared him[4] to the children of men, and has brought into this dark world the light of the knowledge of this glory, with such convincing evidences of a divine truth, and such endearing instances of a divine grace and love in this light, as are abundantly sufficient both to captivate the understanding and

---

1 Ephesians 1:18.
2 1 Corinthians 1:21.
3 1 Corinthians 2:24.
4 1 John 1:18.

engage the affections. This is the true light, which is sufficient to *lighten every man that cometh into this world*,[1] and to direct him through it to a better world. And shall we not open our eyes to such a light? Can we be such strangers, such enemies, to ourselves, and our own interests, as to love darkness rather than this light?[2]

(2.) We cannot but perceive, that there is an infinite distance between God and man, and therefore should gladly believe in one, in whose person the divine and human natures are wonderfully united. The light of nature shows us the glory of a God above us; *as heaven is high above the earth, so are his thoughts and ways above ours:*[3] whence we are tempted to infer, that there is no having any communion with him, that he is not conversable with us, and that we cannot expect that he should take any cognizance of us. Shall we not therefore welcome the tidings of a Mediator between God and man, even the Man Christ Jesus? Shall we not be glad to hear, that this God *above us* is, in Christ, *Immanuel, God* with *us*,[4] God in our nature, *God manifested in the flesh;* the Eternal Word incarnate, which will facilitate our communion with God, and represent it to us as a thing possible? When we look

---

1 John 1:9.
2 John 3:19.
3 Isaiah 55:9.
4 Matthew 1:23.

upon God as the almighty Creator and Sovereign of the world, a being of infinite perfection and blessedness, we are tempted to say, *Will* this *God in very deed dwell with men*, with mean and sinful worms, *on the earth?* But when we look upon the Son of God clothed with a body, and visiting in great humility this remote corner of the universe, which God has let out to the children of men, as a vineyard to unthankful husbandmen, we are encouraged to say with triumph, *Behold the tabernacle of God is with men,* and *his sanctuary in the midst of them for evermore.*[1] We are quite lost in our thoughts, when we come to meditate seriously on the divine perfections, for they are an unfathomable depth, which we cannot find out, concerning which we cannot order our speech by reason of darkness; *If a man speak, surely he shall be swallowed up:*[2] but when we come with an eye of faith to see the Father in Christ, who is both God and man, and are brought by faith to Jesus the Mediator of the new covenant, and through him to God the Judge of all,[3] this makes his glory the more intelligible, (*he that hath seen me*, says Christ, *hath seen the Father*) his example the more imitable, his favor the more attainable, and man's communion with him the more practicable.

---

1 Ezekiel 37:26, 27.
2 Job 37:20.
3 Hebrews 12:23, 24.

(3.) We cannot but perceive the matter to be yet worse—that there is a quarrel between God and man by reason of sin; that the God who made us is not only a God *above us*, but a God *against us;* and therefore we should gladly believe in him by whom that quarrel is taken up, in whom God was reconciling the world to himself,[1] and who is our peace. *You believe in God*, your great Lord and Lawgiver; and do you not believe, that he requires of you an exact conformity to the law of your creation; that since he made you for himself, to show forth his praise, you should accordingly live to his honor; that he who endued you with the powers of reason, designed that your appetites and passions should always act under the direction and dominion of those powers? Does not even the light of nature tell you, that God, who is the *best* of beings, is to be loved and delighted in *above all;* that all the gifts of his bounty are to be received by us with thankfulness, and all the rebukes of his justice submitted to with patience? These are the rules which you know you should have been ruled by: but you know you have come short of these rules; that those affections of your souls have been set upon the world and the flesh, which should have been set upon God only; that the appetites of a mortal body, by which you are allied to the earth, have been indulged, to the unspeakable disgrace and detriment of an immortal

1 2 Corinthians 5:19.

spirit, by which you are allied to the upper world. It is not only the Scripture, but even natural conscience, that has concluded us all under sin. Those who had not the law, yet showed the accusing, convincing work of the law written in their hearts.[1] And will not your own hearts tell you likewise, that you having offended God, he is displeased with you, and you lie under his wrath? If God be infinitely perfect, as certainly he is, he is infinitely just and holy; and as the Governor of the world, is engaged in honor to punish sin, that his law may not be trampled on, and his dominion made contemptible. Do you believe *this* concerning God, and *this* concerning yourselves? and will you not welcome the tidings of a reconciliation between you and God, and gladly believe in him who was made sin and a curse for us, that we through him might have righteousness and life? Was Christ slain as a sacrifice to slay this enmity between us and God, and shall not we by faith lay our hands on the head of this sacrifice, and apply for an interest in it? Shall not the Prince of peace be our peace? Shall not we receive the atonement,[2] consent to it, confide in it, and take the comfort of it, when it is an atonement which God himself has appointed and accepted? When we see that God contends with us, and that it is in vain for us to think of contending with him;

1 Romans 2:14, 15.
2 Romans 5:11.

with ten thousand we dare not meet him that *comes against us with twenty thousand;*[1] it is like setting briers and thorns before a consuming fire, which are fuel to it, instead of being a fence against it; sure we shall see it is our interest to take hold on his strength, that we may make peace with him; especially when this method of reconciliation is not an uncertain thing, for he has told us *we shall make peace with him.*

(4.) Yet this is not the worst of it: we cannot but perceive that we are corrupt and sinful, that our nature is depraved and vitiated, and wretchedly degenerated from what it was, as it came out of God's hand; and, therefore, we should gladly believe in him who is *made of God to us not only righteousness but sanctification,*[2] and who came into the world, not only to restore us to the favor of God, but to renew his image upon us. Do we not sensibly find by daily experience, that our minds are alienated from God, and there is in them a strong bias toward the world and the flesh; that we are not of ourselves either inclinable to, or sufficient for, any thing that is good, but continually prone to that which is evil? And being thus *sick,* from the crown of the head to the sole of the foot distempered, shall we not rejoice to hear of *balm in Gilead,* and a *Physician there?* And shall we

---

1 Luke 14:31.
2 1 Corinthians 1:30.

not apply that balm, and put ourselves under the care of that Physician? If you believe in God, you believe that as he is holy so you should be holy: but you find you are not so, nothing of his resemblance appears upon you, and therefore you cannot expect he should put you among his children, or give you the pleasant land.[1] Will you not then believe also in him, who has undertaken not only to show us the glory of the Lord, but by his Spirit to change us into the same image from glory to glory;[2] and is able to make good his undertaking? For therefore *it pleased the Father, that in him all fullness should dwell,* that *from his fullness all we might receive, and grace for grace;*[3] that being grafted into that good olive, we might partake of his root and fatness; and though severed from him we can do nothing, yet we may be able to do all things through Christ strengthening us.[4] If it be indeed, as it ought to be, our shame and sorrow, that we are by nature so much under the dominion of a vain and carnal mind—no saying will appear to us so well worthy of all acceptation, as this, that Christ Jesus came to *save his people from their sins,*[5] and to *purify* them a *peculiar people to himself, zealous of good works.*[6]

1 Jeremiah 3:19.
2 2 Corinthians 3:18.
3 John 1:16.
4 Philippians 4:13.
5 Matthew 1:21.
6 Titus 2:14.

(5.) If we believe that God is the Father of our spirits, we cannot but perceive that they are immortal, that they must shortly return to God who gave them, and that we are made for another world—and therefore will gladly believe in one who will be our guide to that world, who will stand our friend in the judgment, and secure our welfare in the future state. Do we not find our souls strongly impressed with a belief of their own existence in a state of separation from the body? The thinking part, even of the heathen world, did so. Natural conscience, which is either a *heaven* or a *hell* in men's own bosoms, plainly intimates to them, that there is a state of rewards and punishments on the other side death, and a righteous doom of every man to the one or to the other: but when we come to inquire, "How shall we make the Judge our friend? What plea will bring us off in the judgment? What is the happiness that is set before us in another world? And what course shall we take to make it sure to ourselves?" When we ask "What shall we do to get above the fear of death?" (we see its stroke inevitable) "what have we wherewith to arm ourselves against its terror? From what advances here can we take a comfortable prospect of our state hereafter? We must shortly be stripped of all our enjoyments in this world; what is there that will befriend us in our removal to another world?" Here the light of nature leaves us quite at a loss. Neither the philosophers with their wisest considerations, nor the infidels with their boldest contradictions, could ever reconcile men to death, or enable them upon any good grounds cheerfully to quit this world. *Animula vagula, blandula*, (said one of the wisest of the heathen upon his death-bed) *quæ nunc abibis in loca?—Whither art thou now going, O my poor soul?* Death, with a noted atheist, was a *great leap in the dark*. It is certain, nothing but Christ and his gospel can furnish us with such comforts, as will carry us without the fear of evil through the valley of the shadow of death. Shall we not then readily believe in Christ, and bid his gospel welcome into our hearts, that light by which such clear and full discoveries are made of life and immortality? Shall we not depend upon him with an entire satisfaction, and give up ourselves to his conduct, who has enabled us to triumph over death and the grave, and to say, *O death, where is thy sting*, where is thy terror? Have we not reason to entertain that institution as of a divine original, which is so wisely, so kindly, suited to our case in the last and greatest exigence of it; which shows us the way, through this wilderness, to an everlasting rest for souls; which divides Jordan before us, and makes a path through it for the ransomed of the Lord to pass over? Do we believe that our souls must go to God? and shall we not believe in him who will introduce us, who will receive our spirits, and present them to the Father, and lodge them in the mansions which he himself has prepared in his Father's house? How forward should dying creatures be to embrace a living Saviour, who is and will be life in death to all who by faith are united to him, and who has said, *Because I live ye shall live also.*[1]

Now lay all this together, and then tell me, whether those who believe in God have not a great deal of reason to believe also in Jesus Christ; not only to desire such a Saviour, but to depend upon the Lord Jesus, as every way fitted to be the Saviour, and able to save to the uttermost.

And now will you hear the conclusion of the whole matter?

1. Let us be more and more confirmed in our belief of the principles of natural religion, which Christianity supposes, and is founded upon. Let the dictates of the light and law of nature be always sacred with us, and have a commanding sway and empire in our souls. So agreeable is revealed religion to right reason, and the established rules of good and evil, that what contradicts and violates them, how plausible soever its pretensions may be, ought to be rejected, as no part of Christianity.

Therefore they who, under color of zeal for Christianity, hate and persecute their brethren, kill them, and say they do God good service, or under that pretence despise dominion, resist the powers that are ordained of God, break the public order,

1 John 14:19.

and disturb the public peace, who think no faith is to be kept with those they call heretics, and that it is lawful to lie for the truth; these put a high affront upon the Christian religion, and do it the greatest wrong and injury imaginable. To such we may say, You profess to believe in Christ, but do you believe in God? *Is Christ the minister of sin?* If he came not to *destroy the law and the prophets*, but to fulfill them, can we think he came to set up a religion that should be served and advanced by a flat contradiction to those principles and rational instincts, (if I may so call them) which were prior and superior even to the law of Moses and the prophetical inspirations? Christ came to renew the tables which sin had broken; not to blot out any thing that was engraven in the heart of man by nature, but to write upon the tables *according to the first writing*, and to *add thereto many like words*. If it *became Christ*, no doubt it becomes Christians, to *fulfill all righteousness;*[1] for we may say of the principles of natural religion, as St. Paul does of the law of Moses, *Do* we make them *void* by the faith of the gospel? God forbid; nay, we *establish* them.[2]

2. Yet let us not rest in a mere natural religion, and a compliance with it, but let us, with the fullest conviction and highest satisfaction, embrace and firmly adhere to the principles of revealed religion,

1 Matthew 3:15.
2 Romans 3:31.

and submit to the commanding, constraining power and influence of them. Let pure Christianity govern us in every thing, and both give law to us and give peace to us. Let faith be our guide with relation to another world, as sense and reason are with relation to this world; and then we shall be led into the paths, and brought under the dominion, of Christ's holy religion. If there be any divine revelation in the world, it is in the Holy Scripture, on which Christianity is built; and *there* certainly it is, for we cannot think that God has put fallen mankind upon a new trial, (which he has not done for fallen angels) and given him no new rule of duty and expectation, accommodated to that state of trial. The Scripture, therefore, is that which we are to believe, into which we must search, and on which we must build, for that is it that testifies of Christ. Christ therefore is he to whose conduct we must entirely devote ourselves, and on the all-sufficiency of whose mediation we must rely; else we are unworthy to bear the name of Christians, and wear the livery of his family.

As there is a practical atheism, which they are chargeable with who profess to know God, but in works deny him; so there is a practical deism, which they are chargeable with, who profess to believe in Christ, and yet have no regard to his mediation between God and man: and both the one and the other are no less dangerous than the speculative, and so much the worse, that they carry in them a self-contradiction.

Let us who are ministers make it our business to advance the honor of Christ, and to bring all to him; as faithful friends of the Bridegroom, who *rejoice greatly to hear the Bridegroom's voice*,[1] and to serve his interests; else we do not answer the character we are dignified with, as *his* ministers. Blessed Paul, though he was a great scholar, determined to know nothing but Christ and him crucified,[2] counting all but loss for the excellency of that knowledge;[3] and he did as he determined, for "in all his writings" (as one of the ancients observes) "he breathes nothing but Christ." "Preach Christ, brother," (said the famous Mr. Perkins, to a young minister who asked his advice) "preach Christ, brother." It is the language of all faithful ministers, *We preach not ourselves, but Christ Jesus the Lord, and ourselves your servants for his sake*.[4] It is the character of Christians, that they have learned Christ:[5] but how shall they learn him, if their teachers do not preach him? The whole gospel centers in Christ; in him therefore let all our preaching center. Let us preach down sin as an enemy to Christ, and that which he

---

1 John 3:29.

2 1 Corinthians 2:2.

3 Philippians 3:8.

4 2 Corinthians 4:5.

5 Ephesians 4:20.

died to separate us, and so to save us, from: let us press duty with an eye to Christ, in compliance with him, and gratitude to him. Let us prescribe comforts fetched from Christ, and founded upon his mediation. Do we aim at the conversion of sinners? Let us call them to Christ, persuade them to come and take his yoke upon them, and recommend them to him as the best Master. Do we aim at the edification of saints? Let us lead them unto a further acquaintance with Christ, that they may grow up into him[1] in all things, as their Head and Root. Are we God's mouth to his people? Let us do as God did when he spoke from heaven, give honor to Christ, and direct all to hear him.[2] Are we their mouth to God? Let us offer up all the spiritual sacrifices upon this altar, that sanctifies every gift. Let this golden thread run through the whole web of our praying and preaching; and in every thing let precious Jesus ever have the pre-eminence.

Let us all, both ministers and Christians, make Jesus Christ all in all to us; to us *to live must be Christ:* and *as we have received him* by our profession of his name, we must so *walk in him;* and whatever we do in word or deed, do all in his name, with an eye to his will as our rule, and his glory as our end, depending upon him both for strength and righteousness, and continually rejoicing and glorying in him.

1 Ephesians 4:15.
2 Matthew 17:5.

It is to be feared, there are some even within
the pale of the church, who seem to have some little religion, but they forget Christ, and leave him
out of it. If we come to talk with them about their
souls, and their eternal salvation, we find they have
a reverence for God, and a sense of their duty to
him, which they speak of with some clearness and
concern; they have right notions of justice and
charity, fidelity, patience, and temperance, yea, and
of devotion to God, and invocation of him; and are
under convictions of the necessity of these, for they
believe in God: but when we speak to them also of
believing in Jesus Christ, of their coming to God as
a Father by him as Mediator, of the need they have
of him in every thing wherein they have to do with
God, and the constant dependence they ought to
have upon him, they are ready to say, as the people
did of Ezekiel, *Doth not he speak parables?*[1] This is
a lamentation, and shall be for a lamentation, that
among those who are called Christians, there should
be those found who are strangers to Christ, and are
content to be so; to whom the *Light of the world*
is as a *lamp despised*, and the *Fountain of life* as a
broken cistern; and who are ready to say to Christ,
Depart from us, and, *What can the Redeemer do
for us,* which we cannot do for ourselves? We *pity*
those who never heard of Christ, whom this Dayspring from on high never visited; for, *How shall*

1 Ezekiel 20:49.

they believe in him of whom they have not heard? But *we are* justly *angry* at those to whom the great things of the gospel are preached, and yet they are accounted by them as strange and foreign things, and things that they are no way concerned in. It is an amazing infatuation, and what we may stand and wonder at. Be astonished, O heavens, at this!

(1.) It is strange, that any who are baptized, and are called Christians, can forget Christ, and leave him out of their religion; surely they must have forgot their Christian name, for they have wretchedly forgot themselves. What? a Christian, and yet a stranger to Christ! *Aut nomen, aut mores muta—Either change thy name, or change thy spirit.* Is not the whole family, both in heaven and earth,[1] denominated from him, as having a necessary and constant dependence upon him? and yet he shall be out of mind, because for the present he is out of sight. Shall he be made a cipher of, who is to us the only figure, and who in the upper world makes so great a figure? Were not we baptized into his name; and by our baptism entered into his school, hired into his family, and enlisted under his banner; and yet shall we set him aside, as if we had no occasion for him? If circumcision was to the breakers of the law made uncircumcision,[2] shall not baptism be nullified, and made no baptism, to the contemners of the gospel?

1 Ephesians 3:15.
2 Romans 2:25.

(2.) It is strange, that any who are convinced of sin, and see themselves, as all the world is, guilty before God, can forget Christ; and leave him out of their religion, as if they could do well enough without him. What? a sinner, and yet make light of the Saviour! A dying perishable sinner, and yet not believe in him, whose errand into the world was to redeem as from all iniquity! Is the avenger of blood in pursuit of us, and just at our back, and shall not the city of refuge be ever in our eye? Can we see our misery and danger by reason of sin, (and we are shamefully blind and partial to ourselves, if we do not) and not be continually looking unto Jesus, the great propitiation? Can we read the curse of the law in force against us? can we see the fire of God's wrath ready to kindle upon us? and not be glad to accept of Christ upon his own terms, Christ upon any terms?

(3.) It is strange that any who desire to have communion with God, to hear from him, and speak to him, and in both to obtain his favor, should forget Christ and leave him out of their religion. I hope none I speak to are of those who say to the Almighty, *Depart from us, we desire not the knowledge of thy ways;* but that you will each of you say, with David, *It is good for me to draw near to God.*[1] Do you indeed think it so? Is that your choice? Is that your delight? Is this the thing you labor after, and are ambitious of, that *whether present or absent*

1 Psalm 73:28.

you may be accepted of the Lord.[1] You know not yourselves, you know not your God, if it be not: and if it be, how can you expect to be accepted, but in the Beloved;[2] and that the holy God should be well pleased with you who are unholy creatures, but in and through a Mediator? It is by his Son that God does in these last days[3] speak to us, and it is by him that we are to speak to God; so that we cannot with any confidence approach to God, nor have any comfortable communion with him, out of Christ. If we neglect him, we come without our errand, and shall be sent away without an answer.

(4.) It is strange, that any who are in care about their souls and another world, should forget Christ, and leave him out of their religion. Brethren, you see yourselves dying daily, death is working in you; and you know that after death is a judgment, which will fix you in an unchangeable state of happiness or misery in perfection; you are standing upon the brink of an awful eternity, and are just ready to step in; now how can you hope to escape everlasting misery, much less to obtain everlasting happiness, unless you secure your interest in, and keep up your correspondence with, him, to whom all judgment is committed, who has the keys of hell and death in his hand, and is himself

---

1 2 Corinthians 5:9.

2 Ephesians 1:6.

3 Hebrews 1:1.

the resurrection and the life? Are we not concerned
still to make mention of him, to whom the Father
has given power over all flesh, that he should give
eternal life to as many as were given him,[1] and who
opens the kingdom of heaven to all believers. How
dare we venture into another world, without being
fixed on this foundation? Were our eyes opened, and
our consciences duly awakened, the very thoughts
of dying and going to judgment, would make such
a terror to ourselves, as nothing could relieve as
against, but a believing sight of Christ sitting at the
right hand of God, ready to receive the souls that
are in sincerity committed to him, to *redeem them
from the power of the grave, and to present them to
his Father.*

3. Let us all make it to appear in all our devo-
tions, and in our whole conversation, that we not
only believe in God, but that we believe also in Jesus
Christ. Let our spirits be purely Christian; leavened
with the gospel of Christ, and partaking of its relish
and savor; delivered into it as into a mold, receiving
its shape and impression, and in every thing con-
forming ourselves to it. The poor are said to *receive
the gospel;*[2] they are εὐαγγελιζονται—*evangelized,*
so the word is. What will it avail us in the gospel,
to behold as in a glass the glory of the Lord, unless
we be changed into the same image, and reflect that

1 John 17:2.
2 Matthew 11:5.

light which shines upon us, so that all who converse with us, may take knowledge of us, that we have been with Jesus,[1] and that he dwells in our hearts by faith.

Let Christ be our plea for the pardon of sin, the plea we always put in, and firmly rely upon; let us never expect redemption but through his blood, even the forgiveness of our sins; therefore we hope it is God who does and will justify, because it is Christ that died, yea rather that is risen again; and therefore we hope he will be our advocate with the Father, and a righteous, gracious advocate for us; because he is the *propitiation for our sins*. Let us make him our plea, and he will himself be our pleader.

Let Christ be our peace, and our peace-maker. When our consciences are offended and quarrel with us, when our hearts reproach us, and are ready to condemn us; let the blood of Christ, by which we are reconciled to God, be effectual to reconcile us to ourselves, and let nothing else avail, or be admitted to do it. What satisfied God, let that, and that only, satisfy us; and let that pacify our consciences which will also purify them. Let him also be our peace among ourselves. Let all good Christians, however differing in other things, be *one in him*, as he has prayed they may be: and let him who is the center of their unity, be the powerful cement of their affections.

1 Acts 4:13.

Let Christ be our prophet, and by him let us ask counsel of the Lord, *Lord, what wilt thou have me to do?*[1] Let him be our oracle, and by him let us be determined; let the mind of Christ be our mind in every thing, and in order to it let his word dwell richly in us.[2]

Let Christ be our priest, and into his hand let us put all our services, all our spiritual sacrifices, to be offered up to God, because through him only they are acceptable.[3] By this name let us ever know him, let us ever own him, *The Lord our righteousness.*[4]

Let Christ be our pattern; let our spirits be renewed in conformity to his death and resurrection, and let us be so planted together in the likeness[5] of both, that it may be truly said, Christ is formed in us,[6] Christ lives in us,[7] and we are the *epistles of Christ*.[8] Let our whole conversation be governed in conformity to his example, which he has left us on purpose that we might follow his steps.[9] Let us so bear about with us continually the dying of the Lord Jesus, as that the *life also of Jesus*

1 Acts 9:6.
2 Colossians 3:16.
3 1 Peter 2:5.
4 Jeremiah 23:6.
5 Romans 6:5.
6 Galatians 4:19.
7 Galatians 2:20.
8 2 Corinthians 3:3.
9 1 Peter 2:21.

may be manifested in our mortal body.[1]

Let Christ be the beloved of our soul, and let us make it appear that he is so, by our delight in his presence, our grief for his withdrawings, our constant care to please him, and fear to offend him, and our diligence to approve ourselves to him, as one we esteem and love. Let us have such a constant regard to him, to his will as our rule, and to his glory as our end, that we may truly say, *To us to live is Christ,*[2] and to us living and dying he is gain.

Let Christ be our hope, let him be our joy; and let us make it to appear he is so, by such a holy cheerfulness of spirit, as will be a continual feast to us. Let us see, let us find, enough in Christ to silence all our fears, and to balance all our griefs, and so to keep us always calm and easy. Do we believe in God? Do we believe also in Jesus Christ? Then let not our hearts be troubled, whatever happens to us, but let us be kept in perfect peace.[3]

Let Christ be our crown of glory,[4] and our diadem of beauty; let us value ourselves by our interest in him, and relation to him. At his feet let all our crowns be cast; let boasting in ourselves be for ever excluded, and let him that glories glory in the Lord, in the Lord Jesus.

---

1 2 Corinthians 4:10.
2 Philippians 1:21.
3 Isaiah 26:3.
4 Isaiah 28:5.

Let Christ be our heaven; let us reckon it one of the chief joys of glorified saints in the other world, that they are gathered to Christ[1] there, they see his glory,[2] and share in it, they sit with him at his table, sit with him on his throne. And let us therefore not only be willing to die when God calls us, but be desirous to depart and to be with Christ,[3] to be together for ever with him, which will be best of all.

To conclude. Let that be the language of our settled judgments, which a learned and religious gentleman of the last age took for his motto, wrote in his books, contrived to have continually before him, and ordered to be engraven in the rings given at his funeral; "CHRIST IS A CHRISTIAN'S ALL."[4] And let that be the language of our pious affection, with which one of the martyrs triumphed in the flames; "NONE BUT CHRIST, NONE BUT CHRIST."

---

1 2 Thessalonians 2:1.
2 John 17:24.
3 Philippians 1:23.
4 Judge Warburton.

NOTES

NOTES

NOTES

MAN'S QUESTIONS & GOD'S ANSWERS

Am I accountable to God?
Each of us will give an account of himself to God. ROMANS 14:12 (NIV).

Has God seen all my ways?
Everything is uncovered and laid bare before the eyes of him to whom we must give account. HEBREWS 4:13 (NIV).

Does he charge me with sin?
But the Scripture declares that the whole world is a prisoner of sin. GALATIANS 3:22 (NIV).
All have sinned and fall short of the glory of God. ROMANS 3:23 (NIV).

Will he punish sin?
The soul who sins is the one who will die. EZEKIEL 18:4 (NIV).
For the wages of sin is death, but the gift of God is eternal life in Christ Jesus our Lord. ROMANS 6:23 (NIV).

Must I perish?
He is patient with you, not wanting anyone to perish, but everyone to come to repentance. 2 PETER 3:9 (NIV).

How can I escape?
Believe in the Lord Jesus, and you will be saved. ACTS 16:31 (NIV).

Is he able to save me?
Therefore he is able to save completely those who come to God through him. HEBREWS 7:25 (NIV).

Is he willing?
Christ Jesus came into the world to save sinners. 1 TIMOTHY 1:15 (NIV).

Am I saved on believing?
Whoever believes in the Son has eternal life, but whoever rejects the Son will not see life, for God's wrath remains on him. JOHN 3:36 (NIV).

Can I be saved now?
Now is the time of God's favor, now is the day of salvation. 2 CORINTHIANS 6:2 (NIV).

As I am?
Whoever comes to me I will never drive away. JOHN 6:37 (NIV).

Shall I not fall away?
Him who is able to keep you from falling. JUDE 1:24 (NIV).

If saved, how should I live?
Those who live should no longer live for themselves but for him who died for them and was raised again. 2 CORINTHIANS 5:15 (NIV).

What about death and eternity?
I am going there to prepare a place for you. I will come back and take you to be with me that you also may be where I am. JOHN 14:2-3 (NIV).

www.ingramcontent.com/pod-product-compliance
Lightning Source LLC
Chambersburg PA
CBHW020603030426
42337CB00013B/1195